Dear Mr. Adam.
you are a
Wonderful
teacher.
I will miss you
With dove
Selma

I Love e You

D0933890

1.6.2000. K.L.

FINLAND

SFG

Contents

INTRODUCTION

Looking down at Finland from the plane in the summer, this country that stretches some 1,160 kilometres from north to south and 540 kilometres from east to west presents a blue-green expanse of forests and lakes. In wintertime, the same landscape is completely white. But as the plane begins its descent, you start to notice signs of habitation among the trees, lakes and rivers: towns, a few cities, large areas of rural landscape.

Finland has a total of 56,012 lakes of over 1,000 square metres in area, and 187,888 lakes and ponds that are over 500 square metres. Water covers about one-tenth of the total area of the country.

Finland is situated between Sweden and Russia, and to the north shares a land border with Norway. The maritime borders between Finland and Sweden, Estonia and Russia are over 1,100 kilometres in length.

Nuorgam, on the Finnish border to Norway, is the northernmost point of the European Union, the easternmost point being Lake Virmajärvi in Ilomantsi, close to Russia. Here you can get a special permission to visit the border zone, where the Russian forests are just a stone's throw away.

The Finnish archipelago is made up of beautiful islands of bare rock as well as islands covered with lush green deciduous forests and flowering fields. In the winter, travelling on one of the giant car ferries from Helsinki or Turku to Stockholm that plough through the icefields as easily as icebreakers is a unique experience.

Although Finland is the fifth largest country in

Wood is everything in Finland. It accounts for roughly one third of Finland's export industry

Europe in terms of its area, it has a population of only 5,2 million. Six percent of the inhabitants speak Swedish as their native language, and Finland is officially a bilingual country. The Swedish-speaking Finns are on good terms with the Finnish-speaking majority, and there has never been any animosity between the two language groups.

Finland is not called the country of a thousand lakes for nothing. The water in many lakes is so clean that you can drink it safely.

In the north of Finland, the sun stays below the horizon from mid-December to mid-January, but the white snow and the rays of the hiding sun glowing from below the horizon turn the landscape into a scene from a fairy tale.

Haypoles are the good fairies of the fields.
In the summer around July, haypoles can still be seen on many fields in Finland. They are still exactly the same as they were hundreds of years ago, drying hay for cows, horses and other domestic animals.

Dancer Reijo Kela was born in eastern Finland, in the province of Suomussalmi in Kainuu. Kela's provocative choreography often makes us see things in a new, deeper way. The name of the work Kela has brought to the hayfields of his home province could not be more appropriate; *Quiet nation.*
Each spring, this many-faceted artist prepares his 'nation' for a new performance in order to tell the story of Finns – a people who are quiet and a little shy, and unwilling to always be on the ready with their opinions.

STONE AGE ARTIST

There are over 60 known rock paintings in Finland, with the oldest dating back to the early Stone Age, about 3,500 BC, and the youngest dated to the first centuries AD. Rock painting is a form of prehistoric art that is specific to Finland; elsewhere

such artwork was done by drawing. The most common subject of these early artworks are elks and people. The pictures have been painted on sheer rock walls that plunge straight down into the water, so that hunters travelling by boat could see them. Sacrifices were offered to the paintings both before and after a hunt.

Near Ristiina in South Savo, there dwelled an artistic tribe of hunters who painted on the sheer cliffs of Astuvansalmi Strait, the largest uniform group of rock paintings in Scandinavia. Measuring some 15 metres from end to end, the paintings are a series of narrative images of elks, people, boats as well as palm prints. Some of the human figures wear what looks like antlers; these are thought to depict shamans dressed up as elks. In the ancient religion of the Finno-Ugric peoples, the boat symbolised the ship of the soul, on which the deceased sailed to his final end after his death. The prows of these boats were often adorned with a carving of an elk head.

The paintings at Astuvansalmi were not discovered until in 1968. There are over 60 figures in the paintings.

Rock paintings in South Karelia contain the same motifs of elks, people and boats, but some of them also have birds and snakes. The pictures were painted on the rocks from boats in the summer, or standing on the ice in winter. The images are painted at different heights, enabling us to date changes in the shoreline and the rise and fall of the water level in the lakes. Looking at these pictures, you get a vivid image of the culture of the ancestors of the Finns who survived by hunting elks, deer and bears.

Utensils and tools were adorned with the likeness of the animals that the people hunted. Weapons were decorated with skilfully wrought images of an elk or bear head, wooden spoons were usually graced with the head of an elk. The elk is the most common figure found on utensils and tools as well as in the rock paintings. In a painting at Muuraisvuori Hill in Luumäki, eight men are depicted in a boat whose prow is adorned with the proud head of an elk.

The beautiful virgin forest in the hiking area of Hossa, in Kainuu, also has a well-preserved group of prehistoric rock paintings. Here, too, the most common motifs are men and elks. This far up in the north, the elks in the paintings have no antlers, indicating that elk-hunting took place in the spring, before the antlers had grown. Many of the elks have a red heart, the centre of life, painted on their breast. It was believed that this was a way of capturing the soul of the animal.

All the rock paintings are done with red pigment, which was considered a sacred colour and believed to provide protection against evil forces. The red pigment used for the paintings was a mixture of blood, grease and red earth. Red earth paint was thus already in use in prehistoric times. It was made by heating up ferrous material dug from the ground. Red earth has for hundreds of years been the typical colour for painting wooden houses in Finland, because it gives a durable and beautiful finish. Some 6,000 years ago, Finns even buried their dead in graves of red earth as a sign of hope that life will continue after death.

The first discovery of a rock painting in Finland was made in 1911 on Lake Hvitträsk in Kirkkonummi, near Helsinki, by the man who is perhaps the most famous Finn internationally, the great composer Jean Sibelius.

SIBELIUS AND FINLAND

On December 8, 1865, in the small town of Hämeenlinna, a second child was born to Christian Sibelius, the town doctor, and his wife Maria. Christened Johan

The objects in Sibelius's birthplace in Hämeenlinna reveal as much about the life of his family as about the spirit of the age.

Christian Julius, the boy was called Janne at home, but later he changed his name to Jean.

Jean Sibelius was only two years old when his father died in the typhoid fever epidemic. Grief was soon accompanied by financial catastrophe. Jean's father had never been good at managing his finances, and the fa-

mily was forced to move a house owned by Maria's mother. After the father's death, a third child was born to the family.

Janne went to school in Hämeenlinna, and played in the school orchestra from early on. His older sister and younger brother were also musically gifted. Both the father and the mother came from musical families. Christian, the father, played the guitar. He was regarded as a romantic, authentic, «divinely naive» and good-hearted man. Later in life, Jean Sibelius said: «...everything that is naive in me – however lacking in inner logic – means so much to my soul.»

The home of the Sibelius family in Hämeenlinna is now a museum. The house was built in 1834, and the family rented the house until the death of the father. The museum has a piano, of course, which was also rented when the family lived there. There were also five bird-cages in the house, and the rooms were filled with potted plants. The cosy museum is a good place to begin learning about one of the most popular composers in the world.

Near the town of Vaasa, on the western coast of Finland, stands the former Tottesund Manor, the main building dating back to the 1800s. On June 10, 1892, a grand wedding was held there. Aino, the youngest daughter of Alexander Järnefelt, the governor of Vaasa, was married to a promising young composer named Jean Sibelius. The newlyweds set out

on their honeymoon by boat from the manor's park, but the weather was too stormy and they had to continue their journey on foot. From

Aino and Jean Sibelius both lived in Ainola, their house in Järvenpää not far from Helsinki, until their death. The house is now a museum. The maestro's favourite place was the easy chair in his study.

Vaasa, the couple travelled through Imatra to Lieksa, to the shores of Lake Pielinen. Pielinen is situated near Koli, a chain of wooded hills which is one of the national landscapes of Finland. Since then, Koli has been declared a national park. Composed of the remnants of a once-great range of fells, Koli was a source of creative inspiration for many Finnish artists, Jean Sibelius included.

Aino Sibelius (1871-1969) came from an extraordinary family. Her father, Lieutenant-general Alexander Järnefelt, was also a topographer and an accomplished administrator. Her mother, Elisabeth, was a powerful personality, a good writer and one of the strongest women of her time. She had a love affair with Juhani Aho, the first professional writer in Finnish letters, who was 22 years her junior.

Along with Jean Sibelius, Aino's brothers – Armas, conductor and composer, Arvid, a writer and fearless follower of the philosophy to Tolstoy, and Eero, one of the masters of the Golden Age of Finnish painting – were all significant figures in Finland's struggle for independence.

In the autumn of 1909, Jean Sibelius travelled to Koli with his brother-in-law, Eero Järnefelt. The

magnificent vistas of Koli and Lake Pielisjärvi not only brought back fond memories of his honeymoon, but also gave him new strength. In his diary, Sibelius wrote that Koli was the greatest experience of his life. The paintings Eero Järnefelt made during their trip to Koli are ranked among the most precious treasures of Finnish national art.

The trip to Koli resulted in Sibelius's fourth symphony, which he be-

gan composing upon his return in April, but only completed in 1911. The work was interrupted by other assignments which Sibelius was forced to take on in order to pay his debts and manage his finances. In 1910, Sibelius made this entry in his diary: «Money matters are to me like going to the water closet, a necessary evil.»

Sibelius conducted the first performance of his fourth symphony in

Sibelius Monument in Sibelius Park, Helsinki, was sculpted by artist Eila Hiltunen. It was unveiled on the 10th anniversary of the maestro's death.

Helsinki in April 1911. Although the public and the critics did not quite grasp the piece, for other Finnish composers it was a revelation; like the Bible, it was a repository of stories about the fathomless tragedy of the contradictions of life itself.

Today, culturally-oriented tourists like to visit the area around Lake Tuusulanjärvi near Helsinki. Around the turn of the century, a number of Finnish cultural celebrities moved here and established an artists' colony. Some of them built their own hou-

ses, while others rented homes.

Seeking peace and quiet, Sibelius decided to move away from Helsinki to live among his artist friends near Tuusulanjärvi. However, he could not find a parcel of land on which to build his house, because local landowners considered him a good-for-nothing character with a drinking problem. Luckily things eventually worked out, and in 1904 Aino and Jean Sibelius moved to their new house, which they named Ainola. The house was designed by architect Lars Sonck,

who at around the same time was also working on designing the most beautiful church in Finland, the Tampere Cathedral.

The importance of the wise Aino Sibelius in her husband's life and work cannot be overestimated. The house, Ainola, has been preserved exactly as it was when Aino died in 1969. The grand piano and the waffle irons are still in their places, paintings by their artist friends still hang on the walls. And the door to the study, the maestro's favourite place in the house, is ajar.

The death of Jean

Sibelius is surrounded with tragic mystery. The maestro died in Ainola at the very moment that his fifth symphony, which is considered the most optimistic of all his compositions, was being performed at the University of Helsinki festival hall.

In 1916, at about the time Sibelius finished his fifth symphony, he had written in his diary: «I saw storks. Once again, I heard my own voices.» Forty-one years later, in September 1957, Sibelius was taking his morning walk near Ainola. On his return, he said to his wife: «There they come,

the birds of my youth.» On that cloudy day, the storks were flying so low that Sibelius could see them plainly. Suddenly, one of the birds broke away from the flock, flew towards Sibelius and circled above Ainola. Then it continued on its journey, calling loudly.

Two days later, Sibelius died, while the strains of his fifth symphony were broadcast live over the radio. In Ainola, however, no one dared to listen to them.

Many visitors stop by Aino and Jean's plain gravestone in the yard at Ainola to pay silent homage to the great composer.

Near the old Turku Cathedral, the Sibelius Museum has a great number of exhibits telling about the life and works of the maestro. And one of the most popular sights in Helsinki is the Sibelius Monument in Sibelius Park in Töölö. The 10-metre tall monument was sculpted in 1967 by sculptor Eila Hiltunen.

The magnificent landscapes at Koli in the province of Northern Karelia were the source of creative inspiration for Sibelius, whose compositions often awaken a powerful impression of nature.

FINLAND BETWEEN TWO CULTURES

Since the Middle Ages, the history and culture of Finland have been greatly influenced by the fact that the country is a buffer zone between the cultures of east and west. In the 11th century, Finland was part of Sweden, which had a prominent presence in the west, whereas Novgorod (now Russia) in the east continually sought to expand its sphere of influence westwards, for example by propagating the Orthodox faith in Karelia.

In the early 1170s, the Pope issued a bill stating that the Finns had been baptised in the Christian faith, and were thus members of the Roman Catholic Church. Over the years, Sweden and Novgorod waged a series of minor and major wars over the borders of Finland, until the Treaty of Pähkinäsaari was signed in 1323, dividing Finland into an eastern and a western part in terms of government, religion, and culture.

The centres of secular government were established at the castles of Turku, Hämeenlinna and Viipuri (now Vyborg). But powers and rulers changed, and during the Kalmar Union from 1397 to 1523 Finland was go-

verned from Denmark, although the country was given a similar status in the union as the kingdoms of Sweden or Norway. At this time, settlement spread eastward across the boundary laid down in the Pähkinäsaari Treaty, and the construction of a castle was begun in Savonlinna in 1475 to protect the settlers. Today, all three castles are important venues for various cultural events.

During the reign of the great Swedish King Gustavus Vasa from 1523 to1560, the Reformation was carried out in Sweden, which now became a Protestant realm. Bishop Mikael Agricola, whose statue stands today in front of the cathedral in Turku, already translated the New Testament into Finnish in 1548. The birth of Finnish literature and Finnish as a literary language is reckoned from that year.

History continued with new kings and new wars. For 25 years, Sweden waged war against Russia, and managed to annex some areas. The populace, however, suffered, growing tired of continuous wars, and dissatisfaction finally erupted in Ostrobothnia, where pea-

Today old hostilities are forgotten, and you can use the train to travel quickly and comfortably from Helsinki to St Petersburg and to Moscow.

For hundreds of years, Turku, the oldest city in Finland, and its 800-year-old cathedral have been playing an important part in Finland's history.

Uspenskin Cathedraal, Helsinki.

Between 1939-45, Finland fought valiantly against the Soviet Union, but lost the war and had to cede sizeable areas in the north and south. In Suomussalmi close to the eastern border, at the end of the famous Raatteentie military road, there is a Border Guard Museum with an exhibition about the Winter War. Along the Raatteentie road there are many old battle-grounds.

sants revolted in the so-called Club War of 1596-1597. The name of the war has its origin in the fact that the peasants, led by Jaakko Ilkka, took arms, mainly clubs, against the nobility. In the end, both the Finnish peasants and nobility suffered defeat. The nobles, who remained loyal to the king, managed to put down the peasant revolt, but the new king, Carolus IX, repaid the nobility by executing some of its members for having sided with the wrong monarch.

Between 1713 and 1721 Russia occupied Finland and most of the upper classes fled to Sweden. The Great Northern War, which broke out in 1700, led to the collapse of Sweden. In the Treaty of Uusikaupunki, Sweden ceded the south-eastern part of Finland to Russia. In 1703, Emperor Peter the Great founded his new capital, St. Petersburg, at the easternmost end of the Gulf of Finland. The fortress of Sveaborg (now Suomenlinna) was built outside Helsinki to guard against the Russians.

The population of Finland grew rapidly. During the reign of Gustav III, Finland prospered economically in spite of wars against Russia. Finally, international events halted the development of Finland. Under King Gustav IV Adolf, Sweden allied itself with the enemies of Napoleon, while Russia sided with France. The Russians attacked Finland and conquered the country in the so-called War of Finland in 1808-1809. Sweden was forced to surrender Finland up to the border running along the Tornionjoki River, and Finland was annexed to the Russian Empire. The country was granted the status of a grand duchy, with its own central government administration, later transformed into the Imperial Senate of Finland.

In the 19th century, Finnish culture and the nation's infrastructure developed rapidly. One reason for this was that the Russian emperors wanted to turn Helsinki into a Russified capital to offset the influence of the former capital, Turku with its traditional ties with Sweden. In 1812, Helsinki was declared the new capital of the country, and construction of the town began on a grand scale. In terms of

convened, prosperity increased under liberal economic policies, Finnish-language schools were introduced, and the number of newspapers increased. Finnish nationalism and liberal ideas gained strength.

The reign of Alexander III signalled the beginning of a difficult time for Finland. The appointment by his successor Nicholas II of Nikolai Bobrikov as the new governor-general of Finland marked the beginning of

White wooden crosses at the end of a small, grey kropnitsa in an Orthodox cemetery near the eastern border. Kropnitsa means 'the abode of the soul'.

social structure, however, Finland remained a Scandinavian country throughout the 19th century.

Each of the Russian emperors brought his own set of principles to bear on the government of Finland. During the reign of Alexander II (1855-1881), Finland saw a series of unprecedented reforms. The Diet was

Russian oppression in Finland in 1899. When the ultranationalist Bobrikov received dictatorial powers from the emperor in 1903, he was assassinated by Eugen Schauman, a young clerk at the Board of Education. After shooting several rounds at Bobrikov, Schauman turned the gun on himself.

Emperor Nicholas II

intended to put an end to Finland's special status within the empire and to annex the country to Russia on equal terms with the rest of the realm. Over 500,000 Finns signed a petition which was sent to the emperor. But censorship was tightened, and newspapers were closed down.

In 1891, Sibelius had composed the so-called Karelia suite, the last movement of which he used for the composition entitled Finlandia. In the spring of 1900, the Helsinki Philharmonic Orchestra travelled to the Paris World Fair, where the Grand Duchy had its own pavilion designed by Finnish architects and artists. Sibelius had been asked to compose a «furious» overture entitled Finlandia, but the maestro did not need to write it because he already had a suitable composition. Thus Sibelius gave his own significant contribution to the Finnish struggle for independence.

The 1917 February Revolution in Russia put an end to imperial power, and also ended the years of oppression in Finland. The October Revolution brought the Bolsheviks to power, and Finland was declared a sovereign state in Helsinki. The Diet ratified the Declaration of Independence on November 6, 1917. Since then November 6 has been celebrated as Independence Day in Finland.

In 1939, the Soviet Union denounced its 1932 Nonaggression Pact with Finland. In November of the same year, Russia launched the Winter War because Finland refused to grant the Soviets the concessions they had demanded. In the Treaty of Moscow in 1940, Finland surrendered the Karelian Isthmus, areas of Karelia adjoining Lake Ladoga as well as other areas further up in the north, and leased the Hanko Peninsula to the Soviets.

Olavinlinna Castle in the city of Savonlinna was built as protection against the Russians. Work on the castle was begun during the Kalmar Union in 1475, when Margaret, the queen of Denmark, was the ruler of Finland. Today the castle serves as the stage of a world famous opera festival in summer, hosting stars from the east as well as the west.

Finland now faced the problem of settling the Karelian refugees. But as the former allies Germany and the Soviet Union decided to go to war against each other, the Finns sided with Germany and launched a new war in 1941. A massive attack by the Soviet Army in the summer of 1944 forced Finland to capitulate. The Germans retreated northwards from Finland towards Norway, destroying almost all of Lapland on their way.

In the Treaty of Paris in 1947, Finland had to surrender to the Soviets not only the areas surrendered in 1940, but also Petsamo in the north. War reparations were set at over 300 million dollars, which the Finns paid to the last cent.

Since World War II, Finland has developed into one of the safest and most democratic states in the world, with an excellent system of social security similar to that in the other Scandinavian countries. In 1995, Finland became a member in the European Union, and at the beginning of 1999, it was the first country to join the European Monetary Union, one hour before all others.

MEET THE FINNS

The inhabitants of the twelve provinces in Finland are as different from each other as night and day. As mentioned in the brief historical outline above, Finland has successively been under the rule of either eastern or western powers. This historical fact has also left its mark on Finland's national character, its customs and culture. It is often said that Finns got their brains from the west but their heart from the east, and that the Finns are different from their fellow Scandinavians. They may be a bit shy and less talkative, but once they get to know you, you gain a trustworthy, lifelong friend. When it comes to strangers, Finns like to keep their distance until they have gotten to know them better. At the same time, they are extremely friendly and hospitable people.

When speaking about the Finnish national character, statesman J.V. Snellman (1806-1881), the father of the national awakening in Finland, would often quote a famous line by historian A.I. Arwidson: «We are not Swedes, we cannot become Russians, so let us be Finns!»

In the province of

Although Finnish lakes have no exotic fish, a diver can still find many interesting things to look at.

Åland (Ahvenanmaa), the majority of the population speaks Swedish, and they look at things from a very Swedish perspective. People in southern Finland are more international than the rest of the population, while those living along the western coast tend to be stand-offish and self-conscious. The inhabitants of central Finland are relaxed and easy-going, and their dialect is perhaps the most beautiful of all dialects in Finland. In the east, the influence of Russian and Karelian culture and the Greek Orthodox faith is reflected in the people's attitudes. They are lively and hospitable, and talk to strangers as if they were neighbours. Perhaps the friendliest folks in Finland live in Kainuu: they are modest and uncomplicated, but also the poorest in the country. Life near the eastern border has always been more difficult than close to affluent Sweden in the west.

The population of Lapland consists of the Saami and non-indigenous Finns. Like all indigenous people, the Saami are very unique. One distinctive group of Finns lives in Savo in the eastern part of the country. They are called piällysmiehet (bosses) by other Finns because they have more than their fair share of self-confidence. Their di-

In Finland, only families and close friends go to the sauna together. Bathing in the sauna is an old ritual, during which you relax quietly and just enjoy the soothing heat.

alect can be difficult to understand, especially since it is coupled with an idiosyncratic manner of speech. If you ask someone in Savo if it's going to rain, the answer is most likely going to be: «It may, but then again, it may not.» Your guess is as good as mine!

People in the provinces speak their own dialects, whereas the Lapps have their own language. People from Helsinki have difficulty understanding the Karelian dialect, and a tourist with a smattering of Finnish may be completely lost in the provinces, where local dialects are totally incomprehensible, at least

to a foreigner.

Religion is another important factor which makes for Finnish diversity. Eighty-five percent of the Finnish population belongs to the Lutheran Church, and about one percent to the Orthodox faith. The rest either belong to no church at all, or to one of the smaller sects. Although the number of Orthodox believers is fairly small, they are among the most visible people in Finland, and many celebrities and professional people in the entertainment business have converted to the Orthodox Church.

Every Finn knows how to swim and fish.

In summer, Finns wash their carpets on the shore. They don't do that just to entertain the tourists, but because that's the only way to clean the carpet. This is an age-old ritual in Finland, although today, ecological detergents are used.

Old haybarns are still found in many places in the Finnish countryside. The games played there are different from those played in city courtyards.

The blue cross on the Finnish flag reflects the blue waters of the lakes.

There are about 200,000 lakes in Finland, and about one half of the population spends its summer on their shores. Fish and sausages are grilled in outdoor barbecues. Even late in the autumn, many people still take a dip in the lake after the sauna. But the lakes are also carriageways, with ships carrying both local people and tourists on the blue waters of the lakes.

NATIONAL PARKS - DOORS TO NATURE

The wood grouse, Tetrao urogallus, inhabits the coniferous forests of Finland. The males live alone for most of the year, but during mating time in spring, they spread their tail feathers, let the wings droop to the ground, and make the strangest noises to attract the hens.

There are over 30 national parks in Finland. Three of these parks are run by the Forest Research Institute, the others by the Forest and Park Service. Many of them are popular places for recreation and hiking. Here visitors are provided with guidance and instruction on how to treat nature respectfully, and with information on how to make the most of their visit.

Many parks now feature nature trails as well as information panels pointing out places of interest. There are also more than a dozen special nature centres which are like windows that open onto Finnish nature. In addition to advice for hikers, the centres provide guidance and information about the terrain. Travel entrepreneurs too offer a number of paid services at the centres.

The purpose of the parks is to preserve sites featuring special soils, vegetation or animal life which are specific to Finland. The parks offer many unique natural sights such as rapids and gorges. Also, sites with outstanding picturesque scenery or panoramic views have been selected for preservation. In yet other places, the aim has been to preserve landscapes affected by human habitation and culture, such as slash-and-burn clearings and natural meadows with old buildings. The national parks attract hundreds of thousands of visitors each year. Anyone may wander freely inside the parks, provided that they follow certain rules.

Most parks provide cooking areas and tent sites. Some even boast a camp ground, or well-equipped rentable cottages or wilderness huts. Firewood is provided free of charge.

The first national parks were established in 1938. After World War II, however, most of them were lost as borders were moved westward, although the Pyhätunturi and Pallas-Ounastunturi parks in Lapland still belong to Finland.

The national parks in southern Finland are busiest in the summer, while the northern parks attract visitors especially in the winter and in early spring, when the pristine snow provides excellent opportunities for skiing.

The most popular national parks are Nuuksio, situated some 30 kilometres from the capital, and Oulanka and Urho Kekkonen farther up in the north. Koli has been designated as a Finnish national landscape.

There are bears in several national parks. However, bears are wary of people, they sense their presence easily and either stay out of the way or run away.

Trails winding among ancient trees take the hiker through many delightful settings.

Nuuksio National Park is one of the few remaining wilderness areas in the south of Finland. The park is characterised by all types of protected forests as well as small lakes, ponds and streams, and it is a popular place for hiking. The landscape in Nuuksio is dominated by tall rocky outcrops and tree-covered hills, dotted with dozens of lakes and ponds of different sizes. On the lakes you may catch sight of two species of protected birds: the red-throated diver and the osprey. Another protected bird, the nightjar, lives in the pine forest. Nuuksio has adopted the flying squirrel as its protected species. These acrobatic creatures dash from tree to tree with lightning speed. At nightfall, they emerge from their nests in hollow trees where they spend the daylight hours.

The boreal forests of Oulanka National Park are situated in the Kuusamo-Salla region. In the big rivers, famous rapids and waterfalls fill the air with their roar. Oulanka is also the natural habitat of many predators, including bears and wolves. Karhunkierros (Bear Ring), a 90-kilometre long hiking trail which follows the Oulanka and Kitka rivers, is one of the

The great grey owl, Strix ne-
bulosa, is a rare bird that inhabits the coniferous forests
of the northern hemisphere.
Sometimes the great grey
owl also makes its nest in
the ground.

most famous nature
trails in Finland, with
many outstanding sights
along the way.

Urho Kekkonen
National Park was na-
med after the former pre-
sident of Finland, a sta-
tesman, an avid fisher-
man and a great lover of
outdoor sports, who go-
verned the country for a
quarter of a century. The
park is situated in a magnificent fell landscape,
with many marked trails
criss-crossing the wilderness. With its 2,550 square kilometres, Urho
Kekkonen is one of the
largest national parks,
second only to Lemmen-
joki in Lapland.
(Lemmenjoki National
Park is covered in the
chapter on Lapland.)

Koli National Park is
characterised by wooded
hills and eskers typical to
the North Karelian
landscape. The panora-
mic views from Koli are
known to all Finns. The
highest point is Ukko-
Koli (Old Man Koli),
which rises 347 metres
above sea level. The Koli
landscape emerged from
beneath glacial ice some
9,000 years ago. Signs of
the Ice Age include glaci-
ated rocks with their
characteristic grooves left

Untouched ancient trees stand quietly over fields of cotton grass.

by the melting glacier.

The landscapes at Koli
were an important inspi-
ration in the birth of
Karelianism. A move-
ment launched by Finnish
artists, composers and
writers in the 1890s,
Karelianism was a ro-

mantic national philo-
sophy which idealised
everything about Karelia.
It was also around this
time that Koli first became a popular site for
sightseeing.

Unless otherwise speci-
fied, the Finnish every-

man's right applies also
in national parks. It me-
ans that anyone can pick
berries or mushrooms,
and flowers, provided
they are not under wildlife protection. Of course,
it is up to each individual
to decide whether flowers

are more beautiful quickly wilting in a vase or growing wild in the forest. When you are a guest of the forest, you must respect the wishes of your host.

In Pyhätunturi National Park in Lapland there are remnants of ancient sacrificial sites of the Saami people. The seven-kilometre long chain of fells (the highest peak rises to the height of 540 metres) was a sacred place for the Saami. The park has a total of 35 km of marked trails as well as accommodation facilities.

Koli National Park is the subject of many paintings, poems and compositions by some of the greatest Finnish artists. The first small guesthouse was built in Koli in 1896. Vistas opening from the top of Koli are part of the Finnish national heritage.

In the parks you may pick berries and mushrooms, but flowers and plants are strictly protected. Especially in the north, there are beautiful wide fields filled with cotton grass. The picture shows a species of cotton grass called Eriophorum scheuchzeri.

Oulanka National Park in Kuusamo is a unique river landscape. In the east, the park adjoins the Paanajärvi National Park on the Russian side of the border.

IF YOU GO DOWN TO THE WOODS TODAY...

About one-third of the area of Finland is covered with forests. They are inhabited by about 500 species of vertebrates, the biggest of which are the elk and the bear. In eastern Finland you can also find wolves, and there are a few wolverines in the north. The lynx lives in the forests of southern Finland. And of course, the forests in Lapland teem with half-domesticated reindeer. Badgers, foxes, rabbits, otters and beavers are also inhabitants of the Finnish forest.

The ringed seal is the most endangered seal species in the world, and it is found only in some parts of the Lake Saimaa. It is also the only endemic mammal in Finland that is protected both by the Forest and Park Service and the World Wildlife Fund (WWF). The ringed seal and its

Bears lead a quiet, easygoing life in the depths of the Finnish wilderness.

A happy family of brown bear, Ursus arctos, gaping at tourists.

nesting grounds are protected under the Wildlife Protection Act.

The three zoos in Finland are all worth a visit. At Ranua in the north, there are mainly Arctic species, whereas Ähtäri Zoo in central Finland has domestic species. Both zoos cover a very large area, providing the animals with lots of space to move in. The zoo in Helsinki is a favourite with visitors, especially with families with young children. To get to the zoo, you can take a boat from the Market Square.

You can see brown bears in all three zoos, but in the north and east you can also meet them in the wild. But remember: bears are even more wary of humans than we are of them.

The Finnish national bird, the whooper swan, Cygnus cygnus, is a protected species, whose loud whooping call can be heard from a great distance. The whooper swan nests in the northern parts of Finland.

In the Ranua Zoo there are many half-tame lynx, which is not the same as the wildcat, contrary to popular belief. Some of the lynx in Ranua have starred in the movies. The scientific name of the lynx is Lynx lynx.

The elk, Alces alces, is the most typical forest animal in Finland. It wanders around the forests either alone or in families, and is as wary of humans as the bear.

The reindeer is a tamed sub-species of the caribou. It can never be wholly domestica-ted, and lives half wild on the fells.

Colourful Autumn in Finland

The Finnish word ruska means a forest glowing with autumn tints. In September, when the weather is often still quite warm, something strange can happen. When there has been frost overnight, the whole landscape is suddenly filled with red, orange and yellow tints in the morning. This is a time of the year when many people go hiking in Lapland. But such colours can be found in the south as well. In the parks in Helsinki, the trees and bushes acquire the same colourful dress, as frost wields his brush to paint his glowing pictures.

FINLAND IS MUSIC

Finns are great lovers of music. Aside from their own distinctively Finnish form of the tango, they enjoy all kinds of music. The numerous music festivals organised by this small nation attract an amazing number of people from all over the world every year.

Although Sibelius is the best known prodigy of Finnish music, there are many talented musicians in Finland: acclaimed singers Karita Mattila and Monica Groop, world-famous conductor Esa-Pekka Salonen, piano virtuoso Olli Mustonen, composer Einojuhani Rautavaara, the crazy rock group Leningrad Cowboys – these are just a few examples of the musical talent Finland has given to the world.

Given the relatively small size of the country, there are an extraordinary number of music festivals in Finland. What makes the Finnish music

festivals stand out from others is a relaxed atmosphere with high quality music and famous performers.

In 1969, cellist Seppo Kimanen, who was about 20 at the time, founded the Kuhmo Chamber Music Festival. Organised in the municipality of Kuhmo, which is more than twice the size of Tokyo but has a population of only 13,000, this two-week musical event has become famous throughout the world. The festival programme includes chamber music classics, famous ensembles and soloists, as well as different themes. The event is known also as The Spirit of Kuhmo, which is synonymous with surprises, humour and simplicity. In the Kuhmo music hall, which has superb acoustics, musicians play in their shirtsleeves. In the evenings, acclaimed soloists relax on the shores of the nearby lake, and festival-goers enjoy the music as much as the locals, who put their heart and soul into the organisation of the festival.

In Kuhmo, time is music. Each year, the white summer nights of Kainuu and the down-to-earth atmosphere of the event draw over a hundred mu-

sicians to the festival.

The Mikkeli Music Festival, held from the end of June to the beginning of July, is organised by Valery Gergiyev, who is not only the festival's artistic director, but also one of the most prestigious conductors in the world. Artists who tour the world throughout the

Matti Salminen is an acclaimed Finnish opera singer, whose magnificent bass is often heard on the most prestigious opera stages of the world.

The Kuhmo Chamber Music Festival has developed into one of the world's most popular chamber music events.

When they do the samba, Finns shed their shyness.

year meet each other so seldom that Mikkeli is like a musician's paradise for them. This high-class event is also attended by Gergiyev's friends, including the viola virtuoso Yuri Bashmet, the pianist Alexandr Toradze, who is reputedly the best interpreter of Prokofiev, and many others, who perform at the modern concert hall of Mikkeli.

In a secret location, Gergiyev rents a cottage for his circle of friends. Here, the mother of the chief conductor of the famous Mariinsky Theatre of St. Petersburg cooks plain Finnish food for her son and his friends, and here they are also free to enjoy the sauna and take a dip in the clear waters of the lake – in short, en-

joy typical Finnish summer life at its best.

The month-long Savonlinna Opera Festival draws all kinds of people as well as famous opera stars. The festival is staged in Olavinlinna Castle, and most of the productions are classical operas. The event in Savonlinna is the best-known and oldest music festival in Finland. The first Opera Festival was arranged in Savonlinna as early as in 1912, with the famous Finnish soprano Aino Ackté acting as its artistic director. Modern, large-scale productions have been organised in Savonlinna since 1967.

The Olavinlinna Castle was built in 1476 by Erik Axelsson-Tott, the regent

The national instrument of Finland is the Finnish zither, called kantele, which has been used for centuries to accompany folk songs.

of Sweden, to protect the eastern border of the realm. The foundations of the castle were laid on a rocky island in the middle of a river. Gradually, the town of Savonlinna rose around the castle. The town status of

Savonlinna was officially acknowledged in 1639. There is also a historical museum section in the Olavinlinna Castle.

The Heta Music Festival, held in Lapland during Easter, is the northernmost music festival

When popular street dances are held in Turku in the summer, there are often more spectators than dancers.

in the European Union. Here church and baroque music is performed amidst the snowy fells.

The Avanti! Summersounds festival in Porvoo at the end of June was founded by conductor Esa-Pekka Salonen and his friends, who are still responsible for the programme of the festival.

Imatra Big Band Festival, which takes place around the turn of June and July, is the only festival in the world dedicated to big band jazz. Every year, about 100,000 visitors flock to the Pori Jazz Festival to listen to world-class jazz, both old and new. The Kaustinen Folk Music Festival held in June is dedicated to folk music from all over the world. The Kaustinen festival is a place where virtuoso musicians are seen as well as heard, and the colourful, exotic atmosphere is almost palpable.

If you want to get to know the Finnish soul, the Seinäjoki Tango Festival, which takes place in July, is the place to go to. Unlike their western neighbours, Finns have no royalty to admire, so each year they elect a tango queen and king in Seinäjoki. Many of the winners of the contest have carved a successful career for themselves in the entertainment business. But in Seinäjoki, anyone can dance the tango from morning till night or perhaps just learn the first steps of the dance that is so close to the Finnish heart.

When the Soviet Union collapsed and became Russia once more, a famous Finnish rock group came up with the idea of changing its name to Leningrad Cowboys. They invited the Alexandrov Choir of the Red Army from Moscow to join them, and since then they have toured the world extensively, entertaining people in their crazy hairdos and pointed shoes.

FINNISH FOOD

Cloudberries growing in the northern forests are used to make delicious jams and marmalades.

Finnish cuisine is a blend of eastern and western influences. Scandinavian fish delicacies, pies from Karelia and Russia, and mushrooms and bread form the basis of the Finnish kitchen. Wild berries are used to prepare succulent desserts.

The Finnish food year begins with Shrovetide, when the table is laden with blintzes and roe of small whitefish, eaten with sour cream and raw onion. Many people consider Scandinavian roe superior to Russian caviar. The traditional dessert consists of Shrove buns filled with marzipan.

The traditional Easter foods are eggs and mämmi, a special Finnish delicacy made of rye flour and malt and enjoyed with a sprinkle of sugar and milk. A Russian adoption on the Easter table is pasha, a sweet dessert made from cream, butter and quark.

The traditional Mayday delicacies are mead and fritters, while Midsummer is celebrated with delicious fish dishes served with new potatoes. August signals the beginning of the crayfish season. Finnish freshwater crayfish are among the most delicious shellfish in the world, and when they are in season it's time for crayfish parties with shots of vodka accompanied by ritual drinking songs.

In late summer and early autumn, Finns flock to the forests to gather mushrooms and berries. This way, they can enjoy the taste of blueberries, lingonberries and cloudberries in winter and spring.

Finnish vegetables and garden-variety berries are succulent. The secret is the Finnish summer, which only lasts about three months. During half of that time, the sun shines practically 24 hours a day, and as the potatoes and berries ri-

pen, they acquire a strong, delicious flavour.

The Christmas table is laden with herring in various forms, beet/herring pickle, casseroles made with potato, rutabaga or carrot, and baked ham, although nowadays turkey is increasingly substituted for the ham. The traditional dessert is prune compote.

Finns use the oven quite a lot for cooking, and from the Finnish oven comes some of the best breads in the world. Breadbaking is one of the oldest ways of making food from cereals, a skill discovered over 6,000 years ago. In Finland, the first bakeries were established a couple of hundred years ago, and today bread is baked in roughly a thousand bakeries. Finnish rye bread is de-

servedly famous, especially since medical studies have shown that it can even prevent some illnesses.

Finnish beer and especially vodka are world famous beverages, but some fine liqueurs are also made from Finnish berries. However, the healthiest drink is pure, clean water, and in Finland you can drink it safely straight from the tap even in the most modest guesthouse.

Every province has its own special foods, which are worth trying. Sometimes it may require a bit of courage to taste the strange-looking foods, but often the reward is a pleasant surprise.

There are plenty of blueberries, lingonberries and other berries to be found in Finish forests.

There are excellent hunting grounds in Finland. Tourist companies at the eastern border arrange safe fishing and hunting ex- cursions to the hunting grounds teeming with game on the Russian side of the border.

One distinctive way of enjoying delicious Finnish unripened cheese is to cook it over an open fire. This kind of cheese is called 'bread cheese' or 'cheese bread' depending on the region.

Slowly grilled over an open fire, fresh fish fillets are a crisp delicacy.

A Kainuu banquet table is laden with an abundance of freshwater fish prepared in countless ways: fish pastries, salmon cakes, salted and smoked delicacies.

FINLAND IS GLASS COUNTRY

The better-known history of Finnish glass begins in 1793, when a glassworks was founded in Nuutajärvi. Glass had been manufactured in Finland since 1681, but the first glass factory no longer remains outside history books. In the late

A glassblower inspecting an Aalto vase at Iittala.

18th century, people began demanding bigger windows with double panes, which meant that glass production had to be increased. Glass was also needed for bottling spirits, and to preserve jam and juice. The demand finally led to the founding of the Nuutajärvi glassworks.

The Nuutajärvi works became international as early as the 1850s, when several glassblowers were hired from Germany, Belgium and France. The director of the works was bought from a crystal factory in Sèvres. The accountant of the factory was a certain G.F. Stockmann from Germany, who was such an excellent businessman that he later founded the Stockmann's department store in Helsinki, which is still the most famous and the finest department store in Finland.

The rise of Nuutajärvi glass to international fame was largely due to the efforts of designer Kaj Franck, who was appointed artistic director of the works in the 1950s. Finland was still recovering from the war, and the award-winning designs of Franck and other great Finnish glass designers, such as Timo Sarpaneva and Tapio Wirkkala, helped to spread the word about the country.

Although the glass town of Iittala is not quite as old as Nuutajärvi, it is the birthplace of many famous designs, among them Sarpaneva's acclaimed i-line of modern utility glass articles. All artists working at Iittala designed utility articles as well as art glass, and all have emphasised the fact that their work would not have been possible without the talents of the glassblowers. At the glassworks, visitors can observe the blowers at work every day of the week.

The most famous article to have come from Iittala is without a doubt the vase designed by Alvar Aalto. The vase has a story behind it. In 1936, the Karhula-Iittala glassworks announced a competition for new glass designs to be exhibited at the Paris World Exhibition. The first prize went to an eccentric vase design, which had a peculiar name: «Eskimo Woman's Leather Breeches». The designer was young architect Alvar Aalto, who was awarded a small sum of money. The glassworks in turn obtained permanent rights to the production of the Aalto vase. The factory never published any figures revealing how many millions of Aalto vases it has made throughout the years.

Both glass towns also have museums, factory shops, temporary exhibitions and cafeterias for visitors.

The Finnish Glass Museum is situated in Riihimäki. The objects in the museum were originally collected by students of the University of Helsinki in the 1950s, a decade of exceptional creative talent in Finland. The students managed to gather some 500 items, which formed the basic collection of the museum when it was founded in 1961. The museum is housed in the old Riihimäki glassworks, a beautiful building, which was renovated based on designs by Tapio Wirkkala. A new section was opened in 1981, on the 300th anniversary of Finnish glass.

The Savoy vase designed by Alvar Aalto in 1936 is considered one of the milestones of Finnish design.

SWEDISH-SPEAKING ÅLAND

On the islands there are many hiding places, such as these sculptural cracks of Källskärskannan.

The autonomous province of Åland with its thousands of islands, straits and wide expanses of open sea, is one of the most beautiful pelagic landscapes in the world. The history of its habitation goes back as far as 6,000 years, when hunters and fisherfolk first moved to the islands. Åland, too, was conquered many times in the past. Countries fighting for its possession have included Sweden, Norway, Russia, even England and France.

The Treaty of Paris, made in 1856, stipulated that no armies could ever be stationed in Åland. The League of Nations ratified the demilitarisati-on of the islands in 1921, and also decreed that Åland would henceforth belong to Finland, which in turn pledged to preserve the language and culture of the Swedish-speaking population. Åland has its own flag and its own postal service, which serves a population of about 25,000 people living on 65 islands.

Åland is a paradise for anglers, and sometimes the local fishermen take along amateurs on their fishing trips.

One of the most interesting museums on Åland is the hunting and fishing museum, *Ålands jakt och fiskemuseum*. The exhibits at the grey museum building in Käringsund tell fascinating tales about life on the islands in the old times, including stories about seal hunting and women's important role in the various stages of fishing. On the shore there are old boathouses, bleached by the years.

Åland is an excellent place for nature lovers as well. In summer, the meadows are filled with many varieties of flowers. The bird on Åland's crest is the sea eagle, and if you are lucky you can see this huge predatory bird, along with other protected bird species, hovering in the sky, calling loudly. There are over a dozen

The islands and beaches of Åland are a true summer paradise.

The pride of Mariehamn is the museum ship Pommern, built in 1903. Future sailors practice climbing in its rig.

The islands and beaches of Åland are a true summer paradise.

nature sanctuaries in Åland. Deer can be seen prancing gracefully in the forests, and sometimes, to the astonishment of arriving tourists, mute swans in hundreds may flock the bay next to the airport of the capital, Mariehamn.

Ships and shipping have always been part of everyday life in Åland. The home port of the giant Viking Line ferries ploughing the sea lanes between Finland and Sweden is Mariehamn, which was also the home of the world's largest fleet of sailing ships at the turn of the century. Three- and four-masted barks made long trips to the wheat markets of England and Australia.

The interior of the Maritime Museum resembles the deck of a sailing ship. There you get a good idea of what the life of the sea-going men was like in the past, when the profession was fraught-with danger. The four-masted steel bark Pommern is moored at the quay next to the museum. The ship was built in Scotland and was converted into a museum ship in 1952.

Among the most valuable cultural sights in Åland are dozens of medieval stone churches, many of which date back to the 12th and 13th centuries. The historical value of the churches is enhanced by their beautiful paintings and sculptures, and every church has its own patron saint.

The Åland islands grow stunted pines and low juniper bushes. Juniper is protected everywhere in Finland.

In autumn even the archipelago glows in tints of yellow
and gold.

FINLAND WAS BORN HERE

Food lovers consider Turku Market Hall, which is over a hundred years old, one of the best places to buy food in Finland.

The oldest and historically the richest province in Finland is Varsinais-Suomi. Owing to its favourable maritime climate, the province has the most fertile arable lands in the country, and its forests are dominated by broad-leaved deciduous trees. Thousands of years ago, travelling merchants used to come here frequently to buy furs and fish, and to sell salt, wine, silver and gold. The centre of commerce was the Aurajoki River, which runs through the oldest city in Finland.

Finnish medieval stone churches bear permanent witness to the long history of Finnish culture and its connections with Europe. The Baltic Sea was Finland's link with the rest of the world. In the Middle Ages, new trends in the arts often arrived in Finland on ships coming from Germany. There are over a hundred medieval stone churches in Finland, most of which are located in the south-western part of the country.

From Turku, visitors can take the Tour of the Seven Churches, which gives them an excellent opportunity to discover Finland's medieval treasures. The tour also includes a visit to Louhisaari Castle, the birthplace of Field-marshal C.G.E.

Mannerheim (1867-1951), the famous Finnish general. Until 1917, Mannerheim served in the Russian imperial army. He then commanded the Finnish government's troops in Finland's War of Independence in 1918, served as the commander-in-chief of the Finnish army against the Soviet Union in World War II, and in the difficult years from 1944 to 1946, he served as the president of the republic. Later in life, Mannerheim settled in Switzerland, where he died. Mannerheim is the most famous and celebrated Finnish statesman.

Turku, the capital of Varsinais-Suomi, was founded in 1229. It was the cultural and administrative centre of Finland up to 1827, when a fire burned almost the entire town to the ground and changed everything. After the fire, Turku lost its status as the most important town in the country to Helsinki, which had been made the capital already in 1812.

Turku Castle was built at about the same time as the town itself. John, Duke of Finland and favourite son of King Gustavus I Vasa held a sumptuous court in the castle. In 1562, John brought his young wife, Polish princess Catherine, to Turku. Catherine brought with her a sizeable dowry and dozens of courtiers, who introduced the inhabitants of the town to new and strange habits, such as the use of napkins and forks.

Turku Castle was converted into a historical museum in 1881. Wars had ravaged the buildings, and restorations were not completed until 1993. Since then, the castle, with its 160 rooms, has been telling its stories about important people and events in Turku and Finland. Today, at Christmas time, various historical banquets are organised in the castle, ranging from a Christmas feast for the poor to sumptuous Renaissance banquets, all in the style of Catherine's court.

Aboa Vetus et Ars Nova, Old Turku and New Art, is an interesting museum. It was opened in the early 1990s on the banks of the Aurajoki River, in the grand residence formerly belonging to the family of von Rettig, a rich tobacco manufacturer. When storage rooms for the collection of paintings were being excavated in the basement, the workers discovered an old cobbled street of a nunnery dating back some 400 years.

Although it was known that the site had been inhabited since the 12th century, the discovery of over 30,000 ancient artefacts buried in the ground was an important one. Multimedia presentations and the objects on display allow visitors to learn about life in ancient Turku, or they can enjoy modern art on the upper floors of the museum.

The great fire of Turku, started by a maid's carelessness with fire, burned the entire town to the ground except for a few stone houses. The only exception was Luostarinmäki, an area of wooden homes situated far away from the centre of the town. The inhabitants of Luostarinmäki were poor artisans and mostly first-generation town-dwellers who even

had domestic animals in small sheds. People who had lost their homes in the fire temporarily moved to Luostarinmäki as tenants until they could build new homes.

Luostarinmäki was peaceful and quiet until it was converted into a handicraft museum in 1940. The chief attraction of the museum is its authenticity. The artisans who were still living there in 1940 were allowed to stay, and, after their death, their homes were preserved in their original state. In the summer, the museum organises several demonstrations of the work of the artisans.

Turku Cathedral is the most valuable ecclesiastical building in Finland and a shrine of national importance. The cathedral was consecrated in

the 1290s, when it had already acquired its present form. In the course of centuries, wars and plunder as well as several reconstructions have left their mark on the building. Several famous persons are laid to rest in the cathedral. A part of the cathedral's art treasures are on display in a museum space that is separate from the rest of the building. The surroundings of the cathedral along the banks of the Aurajoki River include one of the oldest parts of Turku, with fine parks and old architecture.

Not far from Turku lies the small and idyllic summer town of Naantali. In 1445, construction of a Brigittine convent was begun in Naantali. The work was supervised by the main convent of the

Finland was governed from Turku Castle for several centuries, until in 1881 it was converted to a provincial museum comprising just one room. Today all the 160 rooms of the historical castle are open to the public.

The popular Moomin Valley is a tourist attraction which blends well into the small picturesque town of Naantali.

Order of Saint Birgitta in Vadstena in Sweden. Since 1924, the call to vespers is heard from the church steeple after the strike of eight every summer evening.

Today, the main tourist attraction in Naantali is Moomin Valley, a park modelled after the Moomin books by Finnish author Tove Jansson. There is a real Moomin House with live characters from the Moomin books, who entertain children and grown-ups alike.

Aurajoki River flowing through Turku attracts many people in the summer.

ALONG THE OLD KING'S ROAD

The lantern room at the top can only be reached by climbing 252 steps. The beacon is operated with wind power.

In the Middle Ages, crown envoys, merchants, post bearers and affluent burghers used to cross the sea from Stockholm to Turku and then continue their way to St. Petersburg on horseback. Manors and inns, taverns and lodging houses sprang up along the road to serve the travellers, who also included kings and emperors. Called the King's Road, it was the most important thoroughfare in Scandinavia, stretching all the way from Norway through Sweden, Åland and southern Finland to St. Petersburg. The road has been recently revived, especially since the old churches, manors and mill communities are still in existence, as is part of the old road network.

The Billnäs ironworks in the municipality of Pohja is the oldest private ironworks that has survived intact to our day. In 1641, Swedish mining master Carl Billsten commissioned the construction of the Billnäs ironworks community on the lower reaches of Karjaanjoki River. Five years later he also founded the Fagervik ironworks in Inkoo.

Over the centuries, the ironworks changed hands and saw good as well as bad times. But in the late 18th century, the Fagervik works prospered under the ownership of two brothers named Hisinger who came from Stockholm, so much so that even King Gustav III of Sweden once stayed with the brothers at their manor. Another king, Gustav IV Adolf, visited the Billnäs ironworks in 1796 on his way to St. Petersburg. The purpose of his journey was to propose to Alexandra, the grand-daughter of Empress Catherine II, but she declined.

Workers' dwellings along the main street in Billnäs have been preserved almost in their original state, and also the main street lined with red houses in Fagervik is a charming area.

The ironworks at Fiskars were founded in 1649 by Peter Thorwöste, a merchant from Turku. However, large-scale industrial production did not begin at Fiskars until Johan Julin, a great merchant from Turku, bought the works in 1822. The Fiskars industry is still owned by Julin's descendants. The name of Fiskars is known throughout the world for the famous orange-coloured scissors produced there.

In 1983, the Fiskars community was bought by the Pohja municipality, which has developed it into a popular residential area for artists as well as a tourist attraction with several museums, shops and coffee shops. However, the chief attractions in Fiskars are the extensive thematic exhibitions organised every summer. Some of the over 40 residential artists in Fiskars also maintain their own art galleries.

The Mustio ironworks was founded in the 16th century to refine rocky ore. Since the mid-18th century (except for a period between 1940 and 1985) the factory with its manor has been in the ownership of the Linder family. The priceless wall paintings and interior decorations in the main house dating from 1792 have been restored with the help of the National Board of Antiquities. Famous guests at the manor have included the Russian emperors Alexander I and II.

There is a mysterious story associated with the Mustio manor. In 1788, King Gustav III of Sweden was staying in the manor when it was still under construction. The king was determined to continue the hopeless war against Russia, even though a hundred officers of his army had demanded that he make peace. The king punished the officers by hanging one of them, but the war did not end until 1790. Since that day, the halls of the manor have been haunted by the ghost of King Gustav III!

The parks and buildings at Mustio are all carefully tended. In summer the manor serves as the venue for popular antique fairs.

The southernmost town in Finland is Hanko which is situated on a promontory surrounded by the sea on three sides and graced with sandy beaches that run on for many kilometres. The harbour in Hanko was known to sailors already in the 13th century, and Hanseatic merchants used to rest there on their way to Russia. Today Hanko is one of the most popular seaside towns in Finland, with a charming town centre and hundreds of visiting leisure boats in its marina.

Hauensuoli (pike's intestine) got its name from a narrow strait separating two small islands just outside Hanko. The islands are among the most important cultural and historical sights in Finland. Since the 15th century, the rocks smoothed by glaciers have served as the «guestbook of the islands» for vessels waiting in the shelter of the islands for the weather to improve. To while away the time, the passengers and captains used to carve their crests and names, as well as pictures and writings, on the rocks. There are some 640 images and original inscriptions at Hauensuoli, including the names of such famous figures as Swedish kings Erik XIV, John III and Gustav III.

Built in 1906, the lighthouse of Bengtskär is only a couple of hours' boat ride from Hanko. The tower of the lighthouse rising 52 meters above sea level is like a magnificent monument. Through the centuries, the rocky island has seen scores of seagoing men

from Vikings to Hanseatic merchants. The sea around the island is riddled with submerged rocks and there are many wrecks lying on the bottom. Russian authorities first refused permission to build the lighthouse. But when a small steamer sank on the rocks in 1905, taking with it six passengers, the tall lighthouse was built within a year. The material of the lighthouse is the granite of the island, and the structure was built by 120 workmen.

Today the lighthouse is a popular tourist attraction. Visitors can climb the 252 steps of the spiral staircase to the round lantern room at the top. The large prism is still functional and refracts the light of the evening sun in a thousand colours. The beacon in the lighthouse is powered by electricity generated by a windmill.

Prior to World War II there were still several families living at the lighthouse. In 1968, the beacon was automated, and the last lighthouse keeper moved to the mainland. Today the lighthouse boasts a museum as well as a small chapel and temporary exhibitions. Visitors can also stay overnight in the lighthouse, go to the sauna and enjoy a meal. The rocky island is barren of trees, but throughout the summer the crags are filled with the splendour of wild flowers.

Bengtskär lighthouse towers 52 metres above the sea.

Big car ferries are not alone in the water, sailing boats are also popular vehicles for moving along the southern coast.

ROMANTIC PORVOO

Old Porvoo is an exceptionally harmonious area crowned by the 15th-century Porvoo Cathedral.

Founded in 1383, Porvoo is the second oldest town in Finland after Turku. In the Middle Ages it was an important stopover along the King's Road, also known as the Great Coastway. Following the annexation of Finland to Russia in 1809, Porvoo was brought to Europe's attention when Emperor Alexander I convened the Diet there. This was an important event in Finland's history: the meeting of the estates was a sign that the Russian conqueror was willing to respect their rights in spite of the annexation of Finland to the empire.

Alexander attended the Diet in person, and a story is still told about a romance between the Emperor and a pretty Finnish maiden named Ulla Möllersvärd. The romance started at a great hall in a gymnasium by the church square which has survived to our day. Along the square there is another historical building, the impressive Porvoo Cathedral, which was built in the 15th century. It was here that Alexander made his promise to respect the religion and fundamental laws of Finland.

Most of Old Porvoo with its picturesque alleys and wooden houses was built after the fire of 1760. The 240 houses remaining from that time are now protected.

Porvoo is only an hour's car drive from Helsinki, and it has become a popular place for a day's excursion among tourists visiting the capital. In summer Porvoo can also be reached through the beautiful archipelago by taking an old steamer named after Finland's national poet, Johan Ludvig Runeberg (1804-1877). Runeberg's home museum in Porvoo was opened in 1880. Runeberg and his wife Frederika, also a writer, moved to the house in 1852 where they lived for the remainder of their life, although Runeberg was bedridden for the last 14 years of his life. Runeberg is the poet who wrote the lyrics in Swedish for Maamme, the Finnish national anthem in 1846. Frederika died at home in 1879, only two years after her husband. The house has been preserved exactly like it was at the time of Frederika's death.

Porvoo was finally placed on the map of Europe in 1809 when Alexander I, Emperor of Russia and Grand Duke of the autonomous Grand Duchy of Finland, convened the Diet there.

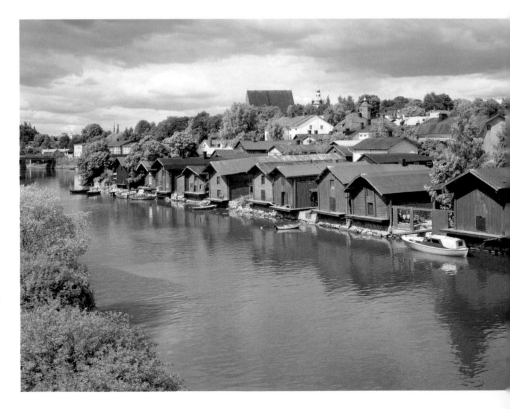

THE HAPPY LIFE OF THE IMPERIAL FAMILY

One of the attractions along the old King's Road is the imperial fishing lodge at Langinkoski. In 1880, Prince Alexander of Russia paid a visit to the lower reaches of Kymijoki river to see salmon fishing. The roar of the rapids, the exquisite scenery and the great catches of salmon stayed in his mind. When, in 1884, he returned to Langinkoski with his wife Maria Fyodorovna, former Princess Dagmar of Denmark, Alexander was the emperor. Dagmar was initially engaged to his brother Nicholas, but when Nicholas died, Alexander became emperor against his will. The imperial couple's sympathetic subjects built the lodge for them and granted the Emperor perpetual fishing rights to the rapids.

At Langinkoski, the imperial couple led a simple life. The Emperor chopped wood with a Finnish axe made at the Billnäs ironworks, carried water to the kitchen and firewood for the stove, on which the Empress

would cook salmon soup. But the housewarming party they gave in 1889 was far from modest. It was attended by the queen of Greece, by the duchess of Edinburgh, and by many other famous people from the Grand Duchy and Russia.

Alexander III had a deep love for his family, for nature and for Finland. When he died in 1894, his son Nicholas II succeeded him to the throne. But Nicholas had no interest in Langinkoski. Empress dowager Dagmar never returned there, and during World War I she donated the lodge to the Red Cross.

The rooms of the two-storey lodge are preserved as they were in Alexander's time. The lodge was converted into a museum in 1933, and present-day royalty visiting Finland often come to the lodge to marvel at the imperial modesty of the place.

On this porch Dagmar, the former princess of Poland, sat watching her husband Emperor Alexander III catch huge salmon from the rapids running past the house.

HAMINA- AN OCTAGONAL GARRISON TOWN

Streets lead away from the octagonal plaza of Hamina, and end in the city wall surrounding the town.

Hamina is a city which has been on both sides of the international border at various times in its history. The city has an extraordinarily disciplined construction plan dating from the 1720s. It is centred on an octagonal plaza on which stands a renaissance-style city hall built in 1798. Eight streets lead away from the plaza. These are intersected by two ring roads. The entire city centre is surrounded by a well-preserved city wall nearly three kilometres long.

There are several museums in the city centre and, since Hamina is an old garrison town, many of these are dedicated to military history. All the more surprising, then, that the best-known statue in the city on Kadettikatu street is not a memorial to some great war hero, but a statue of Varvara Schant erected by a reservist officer training corps. Varvara (1870-1941) was a doughnut and pie merchant who delighted the young soldiers by following them with his wares, sometimes on manoeuvres over open terrain.

Hamina is part of the province of Kymenlaakso, which also contains one of Finland's four UNESCO World Cultural Heritage sites. This is the Verla mill in Jaala, with its foundry villages and the director's mansion, which was converted into a mill museum and opened to the public in 1972. The buildings in the area date from 1885 and comprise one of Finland's few surviving old mill complexes which is still intact. In its day, the complex was an important mechanical woodpulp and paper mill. The interiors and machinery of the mill are still on display together with examples of the work which was done there.

Another attraction in the nearby municipality of Valkeala are prehistoric rock paintings which are thousands of years old.

The Home of the Three Architects

Kirkkonummi is about half an hour's drive from Helsinki to the west. Here, on the shores of Lake Hvitträsk, lies a country home which has passed into the annals of world architectural history. The building was designed between 1902 and 1903 by three young Finnish architects who had won acclaim in international competitions: Eliel Saarinen, Herman Gesellius and Armas Lindgren. A good friend of the architects, the composer Jean Sibelius, had recommended the site when spending a summer there. The structure was log-built on a stone foundation. Its national-romantic style also contained a dash of Karelian influence, as the leading Finnish artists of the late 19th century spent a good deal of time in the birthplace of the Kalevala in search of their cultural roots and soul. Even so, there is a good deal of the English country estate in the Hvitträsk design. The interiors also show the influence of Finnish peasant architecture and of mediaeval stone churches with their imposing vaulted arches.

The most famous of the three architects, Eliel Saarinen, lived continual-

The Art Nouveau country home of Hvitträsk is one of the masterpieces of Finnish architecture. What was once the home of many creative persons, it is now a public museum.

ly at Hvitträsk right up to 1923 when he emigrated to the USA. His best-known American works include the Cranbrook Academy of Art in Michigan. Saarinen became a leading figure at Cranbrook, turning the Academy into the American centre for modern architecture and design.

In the USA Saarinen continued his work with his son Eero, who was also an architect. Until the 1940s the Saarinen's continued to spend their summers at Hvitträsk.

There was an element of scandal surrounding

the private lives of the three architects in their early years at Hvitträsk. Eliel Saarinen lived with his wife Mathilda in the main building, while Herman Gesellius lived with his sister Louise in one of the annexes. After a couple of years this arrangement changed: Eliel married Louise and Herman married Mathilda. Unable to tolerate such impropriety Armas Lindgren moved to Helsinki. After the Saarinens left, Hvitträsk fell into less respectful hands, but it was purchased by the Finnish State in 1981 and the original

interiors of the house were restored. Nowadays Hvitträsk is a museum, the most important of its 32 rooms being the huge studio in which the architects worked together to design a major portion of Helsinki's Art Nouveau buildings. Saarinen's best-known works from this period include the Helsinki Central Railway Station of 1906-1914.

Eliel Saarinen died in 1950, Herman Gesellius in 1916 and Armas Lindgren in 1929. All three were born in the mid-1870s.

THE OLDEST BRICK BUILDINGS IN FINLAND

The folks of Häme, who still have a reputation for being slow and stubborn, were the last to give in to the Christianisation of Finland and the spread of the Swedish rule. The imposed faith, heavy taxes and new prohibitions introduced in the 13th century finally angered them so much that they rose in rebellion. Once again, the Pope had to issue a bill, his dry indignation over the people in Häme becoming heathens again.

The mighty forefather of the Folkunga family, Birger Jarl, the founder of Stockholm and the de facto ruler of Sweden under a weak king, launched a crusade against the people of Häme under papal orders and crushed them. The Hämeenlinna Castle was built as a defence against Novgorod, and the re-Christianised people of Häme were grateful to Birger, who put an end to their slavery under the rule of Novgorod.

Construction on the castle continued for centuries, and the roof and towers of the present castle date back to the 1720s. In 1837, the castle was converted into a prison. In 1881 a women's ward was created, and all women prisoners in

Finland were transferred there. The last inmates occupied cells as late as in 1993. Today, the castle is a museum and visitors can inspect the old cells, which are preserved in the state they were in when the last prisoners left. Managed by the Finnish National Museum, the restored castle has various facilities for arranging exhibitions and meetings, and there is also a cafeteria for visitors.

In Hattula, not far from Hämeenlinna Castle, there is the beautiful Church of the Holy Cross. Along with the castle, the church is one of the oldest red-brick buildings in Finland and a rare cultural site. Work on the church was started in the 14th century. The murals were painted in 1510-1522, towards the end of the Catholic era in Finland. There are some 180 paintings covering themes from the creation of the world to the Last Judgement. Other murals tell stories about the life of Maria and Jesus. The artists, whose names are no not known, were all Finns.

Finland's oldest brick building, *Tavastehus*, contains one of the country's finest cultural-historical museums.

HEUREKA - A SCIENCE CENTRE FOR EVERYONE

Designed by Mikko Heikkinen and Markku Komonen - two of Finland's best known contemporary architects - and completed in 1989, Heureka is a unique, ultra-modern building which houses Finland's leading popular science centre. The centre provides an introduction to the achievements of modern science suitable for visitors of all ages. Besides a wide range of permanent displays, Heureka hosts several major international special exhibitions in history and science. The building also houses the Verne Theatre, a 500 square-metre hemispherical auditorium giving the audience an extraordinary three-dimensional experience. The front entrance of the Heureka Science Centre features a wide selection of geological samples from all over Finland. Its flowering plants are classified using a system which was devised by the Swedish naturalist Carl von Linné (1707-1778) and continues to be just as serviceable nowadays as it was during his lifetime.

Science centre Heureka is popular among visitors of all ages. The centre collaborates with similar centres abroad. Thematic exhibitions arranged in Heureka often attract hundreds of thousands of visitors.

THE WHITE CAPITAL OF THE NORTH

On tram 3T travelling on a circular line through Helsinki, visitors are provided with information about the sights along the way. In the background is the Central Railway Station, which was designed by Eliel Saarinen.

The City of Helsinki was founded at the mouth of the Vantaa River by King Gustavus Vasa of Sweden in 1550. The river waters pass through the Helsingfors rapids just before they reach the sea and this geographical feature gave the city its modern Swedish name. Helsinki did not grow at first, and it was not until Queen Christina moved the city to its present site in 1640 that it began to achieve greater prominence.

Only in 1748, however, did Helsinki really begin to flourish when construction work began on the Suomenlinna Fortress.

The purpose of this stronghold was to serve as a naval and military base to repel any attack by the Russians. The Swedish Parliament assigned Augustin Ehrensvärd, an officer in the country's armed forces and one of the leading experts in the fortification technology of his day, to design the island fortress of Sveaborg. This, it was hoped, would defend Finland against the growing threat from St. Petersburg.

Ehrensvärd confronted some difficulties at first. There were only 1,500 people living in Helsinki at the time and a severe shortage of materials, tools and workers for the construction project. The island itself was home to only a handful of fishermen and their families. Ehrensvärd was assigned a couple of thousand infantrymen to work on the foundations of the fortress.

Before his death in 1772 at his official residence near Turku, Ehrensvärd had been rewarded for his work by King Gustav III and elevated to the rank of Field-Marshal. Saddened by the demise of his old friend, the king himself designed Ehrensvärd's tomb. However, it was not until 1807 that the tomb was erected at the behest of King Gustav IV Adolf. It now stands in a small park in the middle of the great castle courtyard at Suomenlinna.

In the very next year the fortress finally fell into the hands of Ehrensvärd's sworn enemy, the Russians.

Nowadays Suomenlinna is one of the most popular tourist attractions in Helsinki. Its wealth of museums, fortifications, exhibitions, special events, beaches, restaurants and coffee shops can keep the visitor occupied for many hours. The best place to start your exploration is probably the tour guide centre in the middle of the island complex. A visitor arriving in Helsinki by car ferry may also get a spectacular early experience of the fortress as the ferry plies the narrow Kustaanmiekka sound, only a few yards from the fortified cliffs of the old stronghold.

Helsinki Market Square adjoins the South Harbour, which is the departure point for several summer sightseeing cruises to the offshore archi-

On Mayday the statue of Havis Amanda is traditionally crowned with a student cap by students of the University of Technology. The statue is a popular meeting place. When the statue sculpted by Ville Vallgren was unveiled in 1908, its nudity was severely criticised.

Guidebooks for tourists are available in several languages.

The Market Square in Helsinki has been nominated several times as the best market place in the world.

pelago. The Market Square is one of the most popular spots in the city at all times of year. The atmosphere is unique, with fishmongers trading at the waterside and seagulls circling overhead in the hope that some tasty morsel will come their way. Half-tame mallard ducks strut along the waterline with similar motives. On the western side of the Market Square, at the end of the Esplanade, stands the charming statue of Havis Amanda by the sculptor Ville Vallgren. This naked young girl in a fountain was a source of great controversy when the statue was unveiled in 1908.

A short walk along one of the narrow streets to the north of the Market Square leads the visitor to the Senate Square, which is the administrative and cultural heart of the city. In 1811 Emperor Alexander I ordered the complete reconstruction of Helsinki. The city was due to become the nation's capital in the following year and so two highly esteemed men were appointed to plan the reconstruction. Over the period from 1812 to 1825 the Swedish Johan Albrekt Ehrenström compiled a new city plan for Helsinki, and in 1816 the German-born Finnish architect Carl Ludwig Engel designed the imposing city centre buildings, which continue to dominate the architecture of the area to this very day. The Senate Square is stee-

ped in history. An 1849 statue of Emperor Alexander II by the sculptor Walter Runeberg stands in the middle of the square.

Engel also designed the first public monument to be erected in Helsinki. The Empress Stone stands in the middle of the Market Square and is dedicated to the memory of Alexandra, the wife of Emperor Nicholas I, who donated a large sum of money to the poor during her visit to Helsinki. The monument was erected by the city's wealthier citizens as a mark of gratitude to the empress.

The modern commercial centre of Helsinki is the area around the Central Railway Station. Adjacent to the station, the Main Post Office Building houses the excellent Postal Museum - a place of pilgrimage for all serious stamp collectors. Established in 1926, the museum now gives visitors an opportunity to use state-of-the-art technology to explore the history of postal services both in Finland - where official postal services in Finland began in 1636 - and in other countries. The museum shop also sells first day covers and other philatelic treasures.

Finland's national gallery, the Ateneum, is the most highly esteemed art institution in the country. Also near the Central Railway Station, this buil-

ding dates from 1887 and was designed by the architect Theodor Höijer. In those days many artists sought to encourage a spirit of Finnish nationhood - an aspiration embodied in the words of Patria - the fatherland - which appear on the wall of the Ateneum building. Besides various permanent collections and many visiting exhibitions, the building also serves as a venue for a wide range of artistic events.

The Suomenlinna fortress in the background can also be reached in the winter on an ice-breaking ferryboat.

Exhibitions of contemporary art from Finland and abroad are now housed in the Kiasma Museum of Contemporary Art, opened in 1998.

The most popular tourist attraction in Helsinki is the Rock Church at Temppeliaukio. Hewn out of solid rock and illuminated through the roof, the building has little resemblance to a conventional church when viewed from the outside. It was designed by two brothers, Timo and Tuomo Suomalainen, and was completed in 1969. The construction material is natural stone and the ceiling is shrouded in copper. The walls are brought to life by running water which enters through fissures in the stone and leaves through channels under the floor. Due to its excellent acoustics, the church is a popular venue for concerts.

The Finns are a nation of sports lovers. The country has produced several world class ski jumpers, while Finland's racing and rally drivers have risen to international fame and captured many world championships in recent years. The man voted the finest athlete of all time - the runner Paavo Nurmi - was also a Finn. His famous statue, which stands outside the Helsinki Olympic Stadium, has been copied many times by sports lovers all over the world.

There is a fine summer oasis next door to the Olympic Stadium in the form of the Swimming Stadium. Here the water is warm, even in slightly cooler weather so the facility remains open to the public from spring until autumn.

The Finnish National Museum was designed by the same three architects who designed the villa in Hvitträsk: Gesellius, Lindgren and Saarinen. The museum was completed in 1912.

The vaulted chambers in Suomenlinna have many stories to tell about Finland's history. In summer children can take part in guided adventure tours inside the chambers.

Korkeasaari Zoo can also be reached by boat. There you can see real bears.

The Orthodox Uspensky Cathedral.

Temppeliaukio Church is one of the most beautiful modern sanctuaries in Finland.

The Finlandia Concert Hall was designed by architect Alvar Aalto in 1971. It has served as the venue for many international conferences, and concerts are held there regularly.

The Helsinki Olympic Games held in 1952 were characterised by the spirit of good sportsmanship.

The Kiasma Museum of Contemporary Art was designed by the American architect Stephen Holl.

Here you can feel the spirit of Helsinki.

When the Suomenlinna fortress fell and Helsinki capitulated to the Russians in 1808, Finland became an autonomous grand duchy under Russian rule. In 1811 Emperor Alexander I ordered the complete reconstruction of Helsinki, and in 1812 the small town of 5,000 inhabitants became the new capital. At the behest of the Emperor, architects Ehrenström and Engels designed the Senate Square, where a statue of Alexander II turns its back to the Helsinki Cathedral. Today Helsinki has a population of half a million.

From the Market Square you can take a red pub tram which clatters around the city. You can board the tram at any stop along its way.

The Orthodox Uspensky Cathedral in Katajanokka is a beautiful place for silent meditation. The cathedral was completed in 1868.

Orthodoxy in Finland

The oldest and most atmospheric Orthodox church building in Helsinki was designed by C. L. Engel in 1827. This small Church of the Holy Trinity is near the Lutheran Cathedral. Not far away in Katajanokka, overlooking the Market Square and South Harbour, stands the imposing Uspensky Cathedral constructed in 1868. This building with golden domes was designed by the Russian architect Gornostayev. The Uspensky name, by which the cathedral is popularly known, derives from the Russian word «uspenie» meaning ascension. There are some 50,000 Orthodox believers in Finland.

The Orthodox Church Museum in Kuopio was established in 1957 to continue the museum work begun in 1911 at the Orthodox monastery on the island of Valamo in Lake Ladoga, after this area was ceded to the Soviet Union at the end of the World War II. Some of the museum artefacts also come from the former Finnish monastery at Konevitsa, which is also now on the Russian side of the border. Items were also gathered from the Pechenga region in the far north which suffered a similar

The walls of the Orthodox church in Iisalmi were painted by the Russian artists Loupanov and Feodorov, who completed the frescoes in 1995.

fate. The aim was to salvage the Finnish Orthodox heritage from the war and from shifting international borders, although a great deal had to be left behind.

The Valamo Monastery was originally established on an island in the mighty Lake Ladoga by the monk Sergei at the end of the 14th century. After it had been rebuilt in 1715 by

Valamo Monastery at Heinävesi is a living centre of Orthodox culture and religion.

Peter the Great following a serious fire, the monastery with its two thousand monks became an important centre for Orthodoxy in the region. The Orthodox Church Museum in Kuopio provides a unique opportunity to examine the monastic treasures and to explore the significance of the monasteries as places of pilgrimage.

The monks of the Valamo Monastery had to leave their home in 1939 and join in the evacuation of the Finnish Karelian population to the west. They found a new home at Heinävesi in 1940. The monks were few in number and elder-

ly, so that life in their new surroundings was difficult. Since the 1970s, however, there has been a revival of the Orthodox monastic life and nowadays New Valamo, the home of the Finnish Orthodox monks, has become a very popular destination for visitors. The monastery now has its own hotel to accommodate many of its guests.

A short and scenic journey from the monastery brings visitors to the Lintula Convent. This convent was also formerly on the Karelian isthmus, where it was founded in 1895. Like the Valamo monks, the nuns of Lintula were evacuated to Finland by the war. They now make their living manufacturing wax tapers.

The evacuee centre at Iisalmi, with its small domed church, is one of the prettiest spots in the North Savo region. It serves as a Karelian-Orthodox cultural centre, seeking to revive the old culture on the Finnish side of the new international border, and features an exhibition of scale models of some 70 churches and Orthodox chapels which remained on the Russian side of the border

The interior of the modest domed church of the prophet Elijah comes as a surprise to its visitors. The walls and interior of the dome were painted by the Russian artists

In the summer, tsasounas serve as centres of Orthodox praasniekka village festivals on days which are named after their respective patron saints.

Loupanov and Feodorov and their frescoes painted in the 12th - 14th century Slavic style are stunningly beautiful. The walls of the assembly hall in the evacuee centre were painted by the Greek frescoist Andonopoulos in the Byzantine style of thousands of years ago. The beautiful stained glass windows of the great hall were created in the 19th century tradition by the Russian artist Nikitenko.

The term «tsasouna» is used for a Karelian Orthodox chapel or

small prayer house. These are usually wooden buildings with icons on the back wall including an icon to the saint to whom the tsasouna is dedicated. The only old tsasouna remaining in Finland after World War II was built in 1790 at Hattuvaara in the Ilomantsi district of North Karelia. In summer the tsasounas and small Orthodox churches of contemporary Finnish Karelia serve as centres for the praasniekka village festivals.

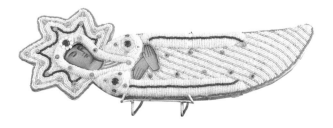

The burial icon of the Mother of God is a priceless relic evacuated from the Konevitsa monastery to the Orthodox Church Museum in Kuopio.

A VILLAGE STRAIGHT OUT OF THE KALEVALA

The Finnish provinces of North and South Karelia have always been midway between the east and the west and so it is here that quarrelmongers from these hemispheres have fought and settled their differences. These territories have changed hands several times, first going to one side and then the other as a result of various peace treaties. Through all of this, however, the Karelian has remained fundamentally a Karelian in character

and feelings to this very day, even though the standard of living of the eastern Karelians nowadays is much lower than that of their western counterparts. The municipality of Ilomantsi in North Karelia has become famous recently because it contains the easternmost point of the European Union. Even before this, however, the area was well-known to the Finns because North Karelia was the place where the 26 year-old physician

Elias Lönnrot made his very first journey in 1828 to gather up the collection of poetry and songs which later became the Finnish national epic poem, the Kalevala. In Kesälahti Lönnrot met Juhana Kainulainen, a local bard, whom he asked to sing traditional songs under the shade of a great pine tree. Kainulainen knew a great many incantations which he sang to the gods of the forest to ensure good luck on hunting expeditions and

Orthodox homes have a devotional corner with an icon, a sacred image painted on wood. Around the icon is a cloth embroidered by one of the women in the household.

Lönnrot patiently recorded these songs from dawn to dusk.

The result of the journeys made by Lönnrot and others who followed his example were the original Kalevala collection of 1835-36, the Kanteletar collection of 1840-41 and the new Kalevala of 1849, which is the one we know and use today and which has been translated into nearly 50 languages.

The two hallmarks of the Karelian character are poetry and handicrafts. The songs of the region tell of life and death, hopes and dreams, joys and sorrows. The image of the Karelian soul bird, which brought news from a greater unknown world, was embroidered on a cloth kept in a special place by the door, next to the wash basin or around the icons in a devotional corner. These textiles, on which women of old sewed their innermost secrets, are now on display at the Ilomantsi handicrafts centre and in the museums of North Karelia.

In Ilomantsi the Orthodox church of St. Elijah and a Lutheran church, beautifully decorated with 116 angels, are side by side. At the bard's farmhouse in the rune village visitors can explore the traditional Karelian culture and way of life. There are also regular opportunities to enjoy the Finnish music of old performed on the original instrument, the kantele, and to hear recitations of Kalevala poetry.

Fine food and wine are also part of the Orthodox faith. The rune village provides all of the delicacies of Karelian cuisine and tourists may visit the wine tower of the local Pelto-Hermann vineyard, which is in a former water tower at Pappilanvaara. The walls of the lift which provides access to the wine tower are decorated with amusing paintings illustrating the wisdom of experience. There are some spectacular views from the top of the tower over the broad, scenic countryside of Ilomantsi, with its lakes and hills.

The stories of the Kalevala evolved in the course of centuries in the gloom of the Finnish forests. The physician and a man of Finnish letters, Elias Lönnrot, gathered these old stories and poems. In 1836 they were published for the first time. A new, extended edition was published in 1849. The Kalevala was an important work in the development of Finnish national consciousness.

RUUNAA – THE RAPIDS AND THE NATURE

Surrounding a chain of rapids in the eastern part of the Finnish North Karelian town of Lieksa, lies the camping and re-creation centre of Ruunaa. The Lieksa River was formerly an important log driving passage, but in 1984 log driving was stopped. The timber structures used for driving have, however, been preserved to enable future generations to study them. The best way to explore the rapids of Ruunaa is to shoot them in a quickwater boat steered by an experienced helmsman. The longest shooting distance is some 30 kilometres. There are still five wild rapids, and while they look magnificent and dangerous, one can shoot them quite safely in a good strong quickwater boat, provided one is dressed in a life jacket and wears a safety helmet. And when even the last of the rapids is successfully cleared, a delicious meal awaits the intrepid traveller in a tranquil pastoral setting. Ruunaa area is also a true paradise for those who enjoy fishing.

The town of Lieksa is situated on the banks of the beautiful Lake Pielinen. Opposite the town stand the rugged tree-covered hills of Koli National Park. In the Pielinen outdoor museum, you can discover the meeting of eastern and western civilisations in the local area, which borders on Russia.

The rapids at the magnificent recreational area in Ruunaa can be explored either by shooting the rapids in a quickwater boat or by walking along the marked trails along the banks of the river. The longest shooting distance through the rapids is 30 km.

KAINUU – THE FRIENDLY COUNTY

Kainuu is one of Finland's poorest areas. Life there has always been hard, since depression and crop failures ravaged the district for centuries. In those difficult times, people were forced to eat bark bread, which is rye bread baked with a mixture of rye flour and finely ground bark of a pine tree. Modern health enthusiasts have discovered the nutritious properties of bark bread and claim that it provides people with the much-needed fibre often lacking in today's diet!

Tar burning came to the rescue of the district's economy in 1800s. Tar was burned and then transported in large tar boats along the huge Oulu Lake to the town of Oulu, where it was sold to local tar merchants or sometimes exchanged for rye flour. This was Kainuu's main livelihood, albeit very labour intensive and often the result of blood, sweat and tears. The process of turning pine trees into tar could take as long as three years. When tar ceased to be in demand, Kainuu's

economy suffered another crash. This state of affairs lasted until the onset of the rebuilding programme in the neighbouring Russian town of Kostamus, which provided work for local men and resulted in a temporary resurgence of Kainuu's economy. Because of the current depression in the Russian economy, the people of Kainuu nowadays take food and clothing aid to Kostamus, and not the other way around. Kainuu shares a 260-kilometre stretch of border

with Russia. On the other side of that border, there is glorious scenery and magnificent nature. Here Kainuu's travel companies arrange safe fishing, hunting and cultural visits.

The Kainuu are among the most hospitable and friendly peoples in Finland, and the entire area of Kainuu is one of the country's most beautiful locations. The Kuhmo Chamber Music Festival has evolved from humble beginnings to a sizeable annual event, and it has made Kuhmo world famous. Kuhmo is also where you will find the excellent Kalevala village, where visitors can learn about the characters and locations of Finland's national epic, Kalevala. Marked nature trails of varying lengths are available to all those who want to discover the tranquillity of the great wilderness. Although it is not an especially affluent region, in addition to its many sites, Kainuu is able to offer visitors some delicious local produce. Nowhere in Finland can you sample tastier fish dishes, which are prepared in a variety of ways and with fish freshly caught in one of Kainuu's lakes.

THE WILDEST NATURE IN FINLAND

In the rivers and lakes in Kuusamo you can catch brown trout.

Kuusamo is a paradise for nature-loving visitors. It is the land of naked mountains and deep rivers set in magnificent ra- vines. It is also the land of great rapids. The fa- mous rapids of Kitka River run wild and free. Some of those rapids are so awesome that it is ad- visable to listen to their surge and to enjoy them from the safety of dry land. The description of national parks earlier in the book mentioned Oulanka National Park, which is one of Finland's most popular. Oulanka is one of Kuusamo's most central nature facilities. The centre of the area's winter tourism is the mountain Ruka, where the majority of local na- ture service outfitters are based all year round.

The best way to cross a swamp is to use the duckboards.

A tributary of Oulankajoki River, Kitkajoki River in Oulanka National Park twists and turns over 35 km.

A solitary fisherman overlooking the mist raised by the sun's warmth.

The wild rapids in Kuusamo can be shot safely with an experienced helmsman steering the boat.

Nature in Kuusamo is delicate

On the border between Lapland and the rest of Finland, Kuusamo is characterised by bare fells and deep rivers running in ravines. In Oulanka National Park the rivers run through mighty rapids, but the landscape also has its quiet spots whose images will stay with you long after you've returned home. They are like artworks painted by nature, and it's invigorating just to look at them.

The busy tourist centre with its many services is situated at the foot of the Rukatunturi fell.

THE COUNTRY OF THE LAPPS

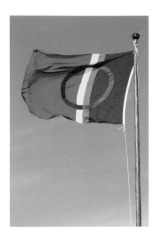

The history of Lapland describes how man first ventured into this inhospitable wilderness, used it as a hunting ground, gradually learned how to fertilise the soil, and later established little hamlets in areas formerly ruled by the forces of nature.

Nobody knows for sure for how long Lapland has been inhabited. Ten thousand years ago, there were people living on the shores of the Atlantic and the Arctic Oceans, as well as on the banks of the rivers that empty into the northern parts of the Gulf of Bothnia. We do not know for sure to which race these people belonged or what language they spoke. We only know that the southern tribes robbed those ancient inhabitants of their lands and that Finns or the Vikings later forced the Saami tribe ever further north. Based on some grave findings and rock drawings, we can safely say that these parts have been inhabited since the end of the Ice Age.

The entire north, or Ultima Thule as the Roman historian Tacitus first described it, was for a long time a hunting ground for both the eastern and the western tribes. Lapps, or the Saami people, were pushed ever further north while the forests and salmon-filled rivers were plundered by the newcomers. The southern culture did, however, spread slowly towards the retreating north. The Second World War brought a great unrest for Lapland, as the northern regions of both Finland and Norway turned into battlegrounds and faced great destruction. In Finland, for instance, there is only one village, Suvanto, where one can see complete examples of traditional Lapp architecture. The rest of the villages and communities were almost razed to the ground by the retreating Germans in the final stages of their war effort.

The Saami language has ten different dialects. The Finnish Saami speak three of them: Northern, Inari, and Koltta. Kolttas are Orthodox Christians: a few of them live in Finland and a few more in Norway, along the Russian border, and the remainder live in Russia, in corresponding border regions.

Saami music, called joiku, contains very few words. It has no beginning and no end. Joiku is a way to remember other people, say the Saami. Many Saami people are very accomplished artists, singers and authors.

Reindeer rallies are held in many places in Lapland.

The Saami wear their colourful traditional clothes also on week-days. The lasso carried over the shoulder is for catching runaway reindeer.

Reindeer roundups are also a test of strength.

The Lapp tent, called kota, has a hole in the roof to allow smoke from the fire in the middle of the tent to escape.

The winter months are not dark
In Lapland, the sun sinks below the horizon in mid-December and does not rise again until mid-January. This time is called kaamos, but contrary to what one might expect, it is not dark but filled with tints ranging from pale blue to pale violet. Lapland's very own bird is the Siberian jay, Perisoreus infaustus, a friendly creature that likes to keep company with tourists.

Aurora Borealis

Among Lapland's most beautiful natural spectacles is the aurora borealis. These days, many Lapp hotels employ a night watchman, who knocks on the doors of foreign visitors when this rare phenomenon occurs, and calls out: «Quickly everyone, the heavenly bonfires are lit and burn brightly!» During the winter months, the Arctic regions are ruled by a blue-grey, eerily quiet Polar night. That is when the frosty northern sky presents different shades of green, white and red and daintily dancing light spectacles that dart up and down and from side to side. Old Saami folk believe that the aurora borealis is created when a fox brushes the snow heaps with its bushy tail, sending particles of snow into the air thus creating lights in different colours. Unfortunately this beautiful legend is not true. These magnificent light spectacles take place at an altitude of a hundred kilometres and are linked with magnetic storms and sunspots. The aurora borealis is a result of an earth-bound electromagnetic shower of particles (solar flux).

Gold in Lapland

Finland's largest national park in Lemmenjoki is also famous for its big rivers, the most famed of which is the 70-kilometre long Lemmenjoki. It is surrounded by mountains which are 500-metres high. Lemmenjoki is an excellent location for the discriminating and experienced hiker. The area's main attraction is the valley of Lemmenjoki. In Kultala of Morgamojoki, there is an information point dealing with gold prospecting in Lapland. Gold has been found in several places in Lapland, and the region has been the focus of two gold rushes. Ivalo and Lemmenjoki are the most famous prospecting rivers. In Tankavaara, south of Ivalo, visitors can try their luck at panning for gold. This is also home of the Gold Museum, which explains the past and the present of gold prospecting. In 1970s, the professional gold prospectors began to show amateurs how to use a gold pan. The men probably decided that the money brought in by tourists provided a more reliable income than the nuggets they could find. Annual gold prospecting championships are also held in Tankavaara.

When a Lapp shaman meditates on the mysteries of nature, the pipe is a mandatory accessory.

THE LAPP MUSEUM SIIDA

In Inari, northern Lapland, there is a Lapp museum called Siida, which acquired a fine new building in 1998. It was designed by architect Juhani Pallasmaa. The museum complex also includes some ancient buildings that formerly belonged to the old Inari museum which, along with a collection of historical objects, tells us about the history and life of the Saami people.

A part of the museum introduces us to Saami domestic industry, which for hundreds of years played an important part in a Saami family's daily life. Old Saami objects were always made for some practical purpose, and nothing was ever wasted. For example, all the parts of a slaughtered reindeer were used. The genuine Saami handicrafts are sold under the name Sami Duodji. Objects are made of reindeer bones, skin and wood. The large wooden Lapp ladle called kuksa, a skilfully hand-made work of art made of willow or birch, is used at campfires to serve up freshly brewed coffee. Lapp textiles are ablaze with the colours of the aurora borealis.

The new Siida museum also houses basic displays about Lapp culture and nature. In addition, it houses a nature centre of the Forest and Park Service, which supplies the visitor with information about Lapland's nature tourism. Saami culture has always revolved around the annual cycle of nature. The museum is situated in a beautiful location on the banks of a lake 81 kilometres by 41 kilometres. According to Saami beliefs, thunder was always worshipped before other gods. The locals call thunder Ukko, which loosely translates as «an old man». One of the most important sites for Ukko worship is an island called Ukonsaari, which lies at the westernmost end of Lake Inari. On this island, sacrificial horns could still be found in 1910. The Reformation destroyed many1 of the artefacts connected with genuine Lapp beliefs and culture, such as beautiful and skilfully manufactured witch drums. Clergymen such as Tuderus, who lived in 1640s, deemed their own beliefs the only correct ones and consequently broke up and burned a large quantity of the drums. The only witch drums spared during the purges can now

The Lapp museum called Siida in Inari is dedicated to the culture and lifestyle of the Saami. Opened in 1997, the museum introduces the visitor to the history of these indigenous people of Lapland. A centre of Lapland nature also operates in conjunction with the museum. In Inari you can still find genuine Saami craftwork made from natural materials.

be found in museums of Leipzig, Stockholm and Copenhagen. Fortunately modern artisans are able to reproduce them as souvenirs for tourists.

THE SNOW CASTLE OF KEMI

The world's greatest snow castle was first built in Kemi at the mouth of the Gulf of Bothnia in 1996. Its fame spread instantly everywhere and it has since become an annual event. The huge snow castle hosts concerts, live theatre, weddings and religious services. The construction of the castle always begins at the beginning of the year, depending on the prevailing snow conditions. Inside the castle, you can sit on a chair made of snow and enjoy a meal in the snow restaurant.

From Kemi Port, a real icebreaker takes tourists on an excursion to the icefields far out on the sea.

Through January to April, visitors can test their stamina in the restaurants, hotel suites or in the church of the world's biggest snow castle in Kemi. Some even go there to get into shape.

ARCTIC ARKTIKUM

On the banks of the Ounas River in Rovaniemi, Lapland's capital, stands a magnificent building where it is possible to learn why life in the dark, solitary, cold north is such a continuous challenge for those living in this inhospitable region. There, one can dive hundreds of metres into the depths of the northern sea of Barents or discover the secrets of the shamans. One large exhibition space in the museum contains a huge arctic zone, which enables visitors to grasp the true size of Greenland, the biggest island in the world.

Arktikum is a window on the arctic world. Designed in 1992 by a group of Danish architects, Birch-Bonderup & Thorup-Waade, this magnificent building houses a museum that is divided in two: the Lapp district museum and the arctic centre of the University of Lapland.

From the end of November until the middle of January, the sun does not rise at all in Lapland. This period is called the Polar night. Around Christmas time, the Polar night is at its most beautiful and the landscape is ablaze with varying shades of blue, lilac and pink. The whiteness of snow and the starlit sky alone make the nights seem bright, not to mention the effects of the aurora borealis.

During the summer, which lasts from May to July, the sun in northern Lapland never sets at all. It is daylight 24 hours a day.

A young skier getting to know modern Lapland and its ski services.

A young Saami boy guards the fire made by the men and watches over the coffee pot, in which real Finnish pannukahvi which has a fine, unique taste, is made.

Driving a reindeer sleigh is not easy at first, because the animal immediately knows when it has a tourist on board and tries to overturn the sleigh. Learning how to handle the reindeer is not difficult, however, and you'll end up with a real reindeer driver's licence to take home with you.

Visitors can stay overnight in the wilderness huts in winter. If you're lucky, someone has stayed there the night before.

Many tourist centres in Lapland offer rides in a sleigh which is drawn by friendly huskies.

You might want to get some instructions, before you ride a snowmobile for the first time.

Lapland with its many slopes and cross-country ski trails is the
favourite region for winter sports.

SANTA AT HOME

The Finnish Santa Claus lives in his secret hideaway home in the border region of Korvatunturi, deep inside a mountain. The mountain gets its name from the three «ears», which Santa uses to listen to the wishes of all the world's children. He has chosen this tranquil setting as his home, so that nobody can surprise him and his wife and the hundreds of elves, who toil away month after month preparing presents. Santa does, however, often perform in various locations such as the mountain hotels and the airport, where he welcomes airplanes bringing foreign visitors. His headquarters are at Santa's Pajakylä (workshop village) north of Rovaniemi. Here Santa has his own wonderful post office, where he meets people daily. You can even have your photo taken with Santa.

In 1998, a new theme park, called Santapark, was opened. It is devoted to the myth of Santa Claus and closely connected with Pajakylä, with a road running between the two. Near Santapark there is Santa's own reindeer park, where visitors can try riding the partly domesticated authentic mode of transpor-

The Finnish Santa Claus lives in his secret hideaway home in the border region of Korvatunturi (ear mountain). With his 'ears' Santa can listen to the wishes of children all over the world.

tation of the indigenous Lapp population.

In December, dozens of charter planes arrive at Rovaniemi, bringing Christmas visitors who want to find out about snow, reindeer and Santa, and who, of course, want to buy their Christmas presents in the shops of Pajakylä. A winter holiday in Lapland is an experience. The many wonderful local mountain hotels offer snow and adventures. In a Lapp landscape, reindeer, snowmobiles and huskies are much more common as a means of transportation than cars.

Santa Park was opened near Rovaniemi in 1998. The park is equipped with the latest technology, and outside there is a real reindeer park. In Pajakylä close by, Santa has his very own post office.

Winter and frost fashion trees into exquisite works of art.

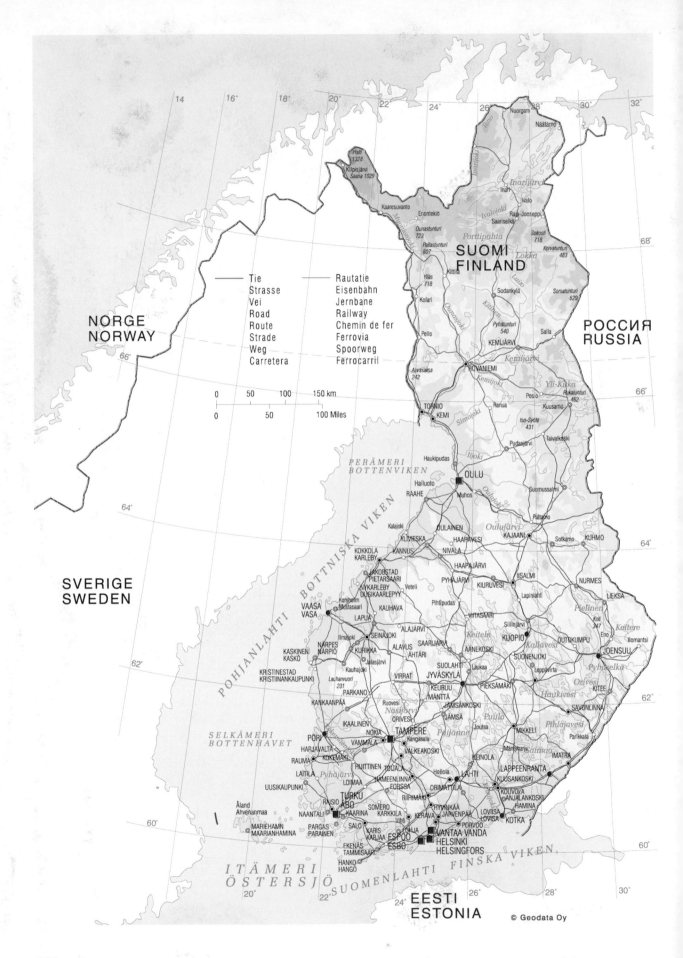